When The World Is Sick

Staying Healthy

This is **our world**.

When Covid came, our world changed.

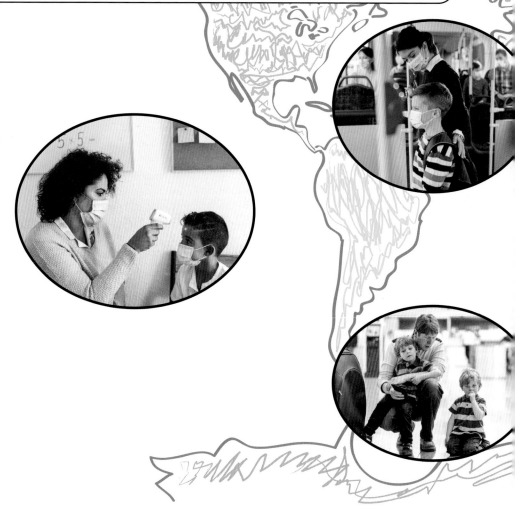

My school was closed.

My school was open.

I had my lessons at home.

I had my lessons at school.

The shops were closed.

This is how

we went

to the shops.

I put a **mask** on,
to go to the park.

I put a mask on,
to go on the bus.

I put a mask on,
to visit my nana.

The planes did not go.

The trains did not go.

We did not go,
on our holiday.

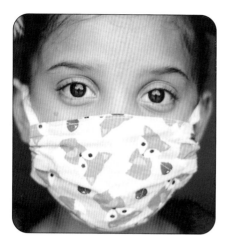

mask

our world